ALASKA II

ALASKA II

PHOTOGRAPHY BY NANCY LANGE SIMMERMAN

TEXT BY HILARY HILSCHER

GRAPHIC ARTS CENTER PUBLISHING COMPANY

PORTLAND, OREGON

International Standard Book Number 0-912856-86-6

Library of Congress Catalog Card Number 84-80125

Copyright ©1984 by Graphic Arts Center Publishing Company

P.O. Box 10306 • Portland, Oregon 97210 • 503/226-2402

Editor-in-Chief • Douglas A. Pfeiffer

Designer • Robert Reynolds

Typographer • Paul O. Giesey/Adcrafters

Printer • Graphic Arts Center

Bindery • Lincoln & Allen

Printed in the United States of America

Fourth Printing

Page 2: One of five frozen cascades spilling down from the Kenai Mountains south of Kachemak Bay, Dixon Glacier presents an icy contrast to the rich autumn pastureland of a Homer farm.

Right: Underlain by permafrost, permanently frozen ground, tundra ponds hold melted snow and rainwater. The thin soil supports shallow-rooted plants like this tussock grass. To the south stretch the perpetually snow-covered peaks of the massive Alaska Range, which separate the vast Interior from Southcentral's maritime region.

Page 6: Decked out in fall foliage, an Interior forest embellishes the Steese Highway roadside north of Fairbanks. Beavers favor aspen and birch as materials for dam construction; porcupines dine on the bark.

FOREWORD

By Lowell Thomas, Jr.

What a perfect way to enjoy this vast northernmost state of ours—through Nancy Simmerman's beautiful photographs and Hilary Hilscher's lively narrative! The only better way would be to see all of it for yourself, but then you would need a lifetime to cover all of Alaska. Having made visits since 1940 and having been a resident since 1960, I speak from experience. I've wandered to its farthest and highest corners as a film producer and reporter, a state legislator and the lieutenant governor, and more recently as a professional bush pilot.

These splendid photographs took Nancy many years of experience and travel to capture, and required stamina and the ability to survive in some of the most unforgiving weather and terrain North America has to offer. Nancy's tenacity is matched by her knowledge of nature, respect for the wilderness, and simple joy of exploring the land she loves.

Coming north from Ohio in 1959, the year of Alaska's statehood, Nancy sought adventure and challenge by accepting a teaching position in chemistry at the University of Alaska. Her love for the outdoors led to travels far beyond the borders of the Fairbanks campus. She became an alpine ski instructor, wilderness guide, and ultimately a full-time professional photographer—one of the first women to do so in the state of Alaska. She camped in the snow at 40 degrees below zero far from any settlement, scrambled up 45-degree scree slopes in summer's heat and mosquitoes in search of Dall sheep, followed the trans-Alaska oil pipeline to the Arctic Ocean, and slept nights on mountaintops waiting to photograph a burst of Northern Lights. Reminiscences of her encounters with bears and visits to Eskimo whaling camps enliven winter evenings beside the wood burner.

I'm reminded of a memorable trip I made some years ago while filming a documentary for the University of Alaska. Cameraman Bill Bacon and I flew from Barrow in an Arctic Research Lab twin-engine plane far out across the frozen Arctic Ocean to a research station on an ice island named "Arlis Two," not far from the North Pole. Our mission: to show what a handful of scientists were doing to unravel the secrets of the Arctic Ocean by probing the bottom, studying the dynamics of sea ice, underwater acoustics, and the atmosphere.

Bill and I were to catch a return flight after three or four days, but it was nearly a month before we saw the plane again. Mechanical trouble and a series of storms kept it grounded at Barrow. During that time our ice island continued to drift towards the Pole and the Russian sector beyond. One of the eight men at the outpost was a ham radio operator. He daily reported our drift across the top of the world. It looked as though Uncle Sam would have to ask the Russians to rescue us, since we were near the ultimate range of our supply plane. Our plight became an international news story.

Bill and I pitched in on the many chores required to keep us all alive—cutting and hauling blocks of snow to melt for water and tinkering with the oil stoves that kept our prefab huts warm in the minus 30-degree temperatures outside. Wandering out across the pack ice, we saw polar bears from time to time. One night we were awakened by the crash of glass; in the flashlight's beam a shaggy white head peered with curiosity through the broken window. We hollered at the bear and opened the door to fire a rifle shot into the air; luckily that scared him away. Eventually our plane made it back, ending a fairly routine trip that turned into an unforgettable adventure.

Much of Alaska is accessible only by small bush plane, such as my single-engine Helio Courier with its combination wheels and skis. I flew Nancy and two of her friends up the Ruth Glacier and into the Don Sheldon Amphitheater near the base of Mount McKinley. There they tented out for a week while she took some of the photos in this book. Flying near Mount McKinley is always an adventure. Landings on snow-clad glaciers to pick up mountain climbers are particularly exciting because of the many variables and uncertainties: clouds and wind, slope of the glacier, snow-bridged crevasses, and deep snow. You must be prepared to camp out for a while if the weather closes in or dig out a bogged-down plane and pack a takeoff strip with snowshoes or skis. More than once I've curled up for the night in the back of the plane high on a lonely glacier, waiting for the weather to break.

In this book is a glimpse of Alaska through the eyes of a top photographer and through the words of a talented writer who tells us much about the cultural and economic change since 1970. Fond memories will engulf those who know Alaska; the arm-chair traveler will wonder at the magnificence and abundant beauty of the 49th State.

Above: Home to more than half the state's half million residents, the two thousand-square-mile Municipality of Anchorage features skyscrapers like the Hunt Building. Some office buildings rise next to historic log cabins. Long a crossroads for Native trade, the inlet's anchorage was used by gold miners around the turn of the century. In 1914, it became the construction headquarters for the Alaska Railroad. Six years later, Anchorage incorporated as a city. *Right:* Moose's Tooth Ridge, a remote but popular destination for rock-climbing enthusiasts, looms behind a tributary glacier of Ruth Glacier in Denali National Park.

Left: The only caribou herds in the United States roam mainly in Alaska's Arctic and Interior regions. Before the fall mating season, velvet covers the antlers which crown this bull. Each year, herds migrate hundreds of miles to find sufficient forage: leaves, grass, sedge, and lichens or "reindeer moss." *Above:* The midsummer blossoms of the wild geranium or northern cranebill splash lavendar patches across coastal areas from Southeast to Western Alaska. *Overleaf:* The Wickersham Wall of North America's tallest peak, majestic Mount McKinley, gleams in the alpenglow of an August sunset. Braided Thorofare River originates in glaciers in the Alaska Range.

Above: Harbors lie in the center of town in Wrangell and most other communities in Southeast, whose one thousand islands and steep terrain make a highway network impractical. Economies based on fishing and logging add to the marine orientation of the 540-mile long region. *Right:* An unnamed tundra pond in the Ipnelivik River Valley reflects the Arctic summer sky. The Ipnelivik River flows into the Noatak River which winds more than three hundred and fifty miles through protected wilderness parklands. Numerous features in Alaska's wilderness have no official names.

Left: In 1926, Benny Benson, an orphaned Aleut boy, won the contest among Alaskan schoolchildren with his design for the new territory's flag. His simple, memorable image — the seven gold stars of the Big Dipper constellation plus the North Star on a blue field—now symbolizes the 49th State and adorns the funnels of Alaska Marine Highway System ferries. *Above:* A member of Denali National Park and Preserve's bruin population *(Ursus arctos)* takes advantage of a sturdy sign. Scientists have begun to classify Alaska's numerous brown and grizzly bears as the same species.

Above: Ranging from native clay pottery to watercolor scenes on Kachemak Bay driftwood, the work of local artists goes on display in Homer's gift shops along with more traditional souvenir fare. *Right:* For centuries, Athabaskan Indians have dried strips of Yukon River salmon during summer's sunshine. This was their insurance against hunger for both people and sled dogs during the long winter. *Overleaf:* Turnagain Arm's powerful incoming bore tide pushes a wall of water up the forty-mile-long Southcentral fjord. While one to two-foot-high bores are common here, they may occasionally reach six feet in height.

When I returned to Alaska after sixteen years
Outside, *the first thing that struck me was the
quality of light. It made me remember something
deep inside I thought I'd forgotten. How to
describe that? It's harder to talk about the feeling
of a certain kind of light on a mountainside than it
is to feel the tears in your eyes when you see it.*
                              Alaskan Born in Fairbanks

I first discovered it when I was six: the world *Outside* is different. When I said "Outside" *Outside,* no one knew what I meant. To Alaskans, *Outside,* spelled with a capital *O,* means any place outside of Alaska, usually "the Lower 48" or the continental United States. The expression captures the Alaskan frame of reference: Alaska—the Great Land, the Last Frontier—forms the center of the world . . . the rest is *Outside.*

Our attitude seems to spring, historically, from the land itself: vast, unknown, stunningly beautiful and wild, exotic, challenging, remote. Alaska so captivates the attention, we readily find it the most fascinating topic of conversation. Even as we move into the international mainstream via the economy, transportation, and communication, Alaska—to Alaskans—tends to remain the hub. Along with this view thrives a sense of specialness, of uniqueness—a feeling of being truly Home. A Matanuska Valley author of six books on the 49th State declares, "Alaska translates into an open smile and warm handclasp".

But neither the terminology nor the attitude accounted for my awareness about *Outside* at age six. It was not the fact that it took six or more hours aboard an airplane to get from Anchorage to Seattle. Like most Alaskan children, I had grown up flying. Distances of many hours or days seemed normal to me.

Superimpose a map of Alaska onto one of the United States, and it stretches from Florida to California, from Texas to the Canadian border. Cut Alaska's 586,000-square miles in half and Texas would become the *third* largest state. Between Ketchikan at the tip of Southeastern and our westernmost point, Attu Island, lie more than twenty-two hundred miles. (The international dateline bends far out around the Aleutian Chain to include all of Alaska in today.) Straight north to south, Alaska reaches nearly eleven hundred miles, and shares a partly meandering fifteen hundred-mile eastern border with Canada. Back in 1955, it took two days to drive from Anchorage to the nearest major city, Fairbanks, which is also the state's second largest urban center.

Long distances did not tell me *Outside* is different. But the experience of any roads at all makes the Lower 48 totally unique for many kids from Alaska's several hundred villages, unconnected by highway to anywhere else. Children who live in Southeast have a similar perspective. As one woman who grew up in Sitka on Baranof Island put it, "*Outside,* you could drive for more than an hour in one direction, and not reach the end of the road. Plus, you could *drive* to other cities". Alaska's capital, Juneau, can be reached only by plane and boat. Glaciers and mountains block road building to this mainland community.

We saw some deer by the side of the road in Washington State, so I did not realize that most places in America do not have wild animals roaming freely. I was accustomed to spotting moose (sometimes in our back yard), bear, beaver, mountain sheep and goats, plus occasional wolves, caribou, and foxes. Nor was it the escalators in stores that truly made *Outside* different, although those were unique for me.

So what made it different out there?

The light. Or rather, the lack of light. Here it was, the middle of summer *Outside* — and it became dark at night! With all the certainty of a six year old, I *knew* that Anyone Who Knew Anything About The World knew that summertime means daylight. It gets dark in the *winter.*

As I have grown up, I have come to understand many more things which make Alaska different from the rest of the world.

Some will continue to set Alaska uniquely apart when the babies of today begin comparing their world with *Outside.* And some will exist as memories for their parents, like many things I took for granted as recently as ten years ago.

Of course, countless changes have been evolving, with the roots of those changes reaching back decades and centuries. Alaska became America's "First Frontier" with the migration of people over the Bering Sea land bridge from Asia fifteen thousand to forty thousand years ago. Alaska's recorded history looks like yesterday to Americans—and like only this morning to Europeans and Asians. But since 1970, Alaska has experienced more dramatic change overall than in any other period: changing life-styles, the Alaska Native Land Claims Settlement Act, the pipeline, the development of natural resources, and the Alaska National Interest Lands Conservation Act. Simultaneously, our visions of the future are changing to include new technology and reawakened inner values.

It is easy to make judgments about new versus old, to want things to stay the same and not change. But as one Tlingit Indian man puts it, "Once you take on something new, *you* change. You can't just go back to old ways because you are different too. It's what you do — what you keep as value from old times and how you put that into today that counts".

With fewer than half a million people, Alaska is among the states with the fewest number of residents. If Manhattan Island's population density matched ours, seventeen people would live there. Yet, since the mid-1970s, the number of people in the 49th State has been growing at one of the country's fastest rates. It is a standing joke that every newcomer thinks no one *else* should be allowed to move to Alaska.

We who live here see fewer familiar faces everywhere as we travel. More people mean more change: more needs and wants; more cars, roads, houses; more stores, theaters, art galleries; more ideas, opportunities, possibilities. Alaska heading into the last years of the twentieth century fairly bursts with aliveness. With the vitality of a teen-ager, Alaska is changing, growing, getting to know itself, deciding who it is and where it fits in the world. Alaskans know we have something special to call our own, something special to share and contribute.

The word Alaska comes from the Aleut *Alashka,* meaning Great Land. Many superlatives beyond mere size distinguish Alaska among the states. It has ten rivers over three hundred miles long, three million lakes larger than twenty acres, more than half of the world's glaciers, and nineteen mountains higher than fourteen-thousand feet, including North America's tallest peak, awesome Mount McKinley, which thrusts 20,320 feet above sea level.

Alaska has places with more precipitation than anywhere in the forty-eight continental states — more than two hundred and fifty inches fall each year at MacLeod Harbor, on Montague Island— and places with close to the least—only about five inches fall each year at Point Barrow. Geologically, Alaska has a lot going on: more than half the state is seismically active, with earthquakes (more than 10 percent of the world's tremors occur here) and extensive volcanic eruptions. Permafrost — permanently frozen ground—lies under much of Alaska, and about 70 percent of the state is treeless. In fact, of all the states, Alaska supports the fewest number of tree species: just thirty-three.

What are Alaska's climate and geography *really* like? One might as well try to describe in one word the climate and geography of America. Think of Alaska as five states in one, each of the five as distinct and separate as New Mexico is from New Hampshire, as the Dakotas from the Carolinas.

Starting at the bottom of the state, the Gulf of Alaska stretches in an arc from the southern tip of the Southeastern panhandle region on the east, around the mid-gulf region of Southcentral and west, to the base of the Alaska Peninsula. The Southwest region includes both the Peninsula and the Aleutian Islands. While Alaskans often distinguish politically between Southeast and Southcentral, the two regions share many topographic features: snow-capped mountains plunging into gray blue fjords; dense forests;

heavy precipitation; ice-free salt water year-round south of Anchorage. Southcentral's inland regions are drier and cooler with sparser vegetation.

The massive Alaska Range—the northern extension of the mighty Rocky Mountains—strides across Alaska's lower third in a southwesterly march. This cordillera separates the Gulf regions from the Interior and becomes, eventually, the Aleutian Range. It is the tops of these mountains which form the thousand-mile-long Aleutian Islands that divide the Bering Sea from the Pacific Ocean. Spurs of the Alaska Range—the Chugach and Kenai Mountains—extend like fingers into Southcentral, while other spurs—the Saint Elias and Coastal Ranges—extend into Southeast.

Bordered on the north by the Brooks Range, to the east by Canada, and to the west by the coastal land of Western Alaska, the Interior lies in a broad swath across Alaska's mid-section. Its plains, hills, and low, rolling mountains receive relatively little rainfall or snow and experience the state's greatest extremes of temperature: frequently, the mercury rises into the Fahrenheit nineties on a summer day and plunges into the minus sixties on a winter night.

A maritime climate characterizes the treeless mountains of the Alaska Peninsula and the Aleutians: year-round wind, nearly constant precipitation, fog, and an annual temperature range between thirty and fifty-five degrees—a spread of only twenty-five degrees. The flat tundra plains of the Western Alaska region stretch from the top of the Alaska Peninsula north across the Seward Peninsula to the northwestern corner of Alaska on the Chukchi Sea. Marked by frequent clouds, this region has light precipitation and cool temperatures; in winter, the northern three-quarters of the coastline is ice-locked.

Across the upper third of the state lies the Arctic Circle. This imaginary line marks the southernmost latitude at which the sun does not set on the summer solstice or rise on the winter solstice. It is approximately 66° 33' north latitude. Above this latitude lies the Arctic Region which is comprised of the Brooks Range and the North Slope. The North Slope begins on the north side of the Range, dropping gradually toward the Arctic Ocean which is about three hundred miles away. Here it is cold year-round: summer temperatures often dip below freezing; winter lasts nine months. Little precipitation falls on the flat Arctic tundra, and ice masses remain in the ocean throughout the summer.

> *This country forces you to be more in line with nature than anywhere Outside. There, it's so much easier to be insulated from the elements and the seasonal changes. Here, I think you have to respond to the weather, and to the light.*
>
> *Social Services Worker in the Aleutians*

Anchorage lies at sixty-one degrees north latitude, along with the southern tip of Greenland, Helsinki, Oslo, and Leningrad. Here, the sun shines for more than nineteen hours a day during June, and night is a gentle twilight. Kids ride bikes and fly kites in the 10 P.M. sunshine. More than one adult visiting the North Country for the first time has had the strange sensation of walking out of a bar at 3 or 4 A.M. into full daylight. Two hundred and sixty miles north, the people of Fairbanks celebrate the summer solstice with an annual "Midnight Sun Baseball Game" which starts at 10:30 P.M. There is no need for stadium lights on clear evenings.

At Barrow, five hundred miles north of Fairbanks, the sun does not set on the northernmost town in the United States from mid-May through early August. Winter brings the reverse: from mid-November through early January, a silvery blue twilight brightens two hours each mid-day. South of the Alaska Range, however, the cold, pale winter sun shines a minimum of five and a half hours each day, with several hours of twilight before and afterward.

Fall through spring, clear night skies feature God's own light show: the hauntingly awesome Northern Lights. Some Eskimo people called them torches marking the way to heaven for departed souls. Today we call them bursts of electricity which result when particles from the sun hit earth's atmosphere. Standing out beneath their undulating red curtains, eerie bluish green spirals, and pulsing yellow streaks, it is easy to imagine the heavenly journey those lucky souls get to make.

Between the extremes of summer and winter, all nature races to keep pace with the light: vegetation buds and bursts into blossom with snow still on the ground. By August, the fireweed blooms only at the top of its stalk, dissolving within days into seed-filled cotton which blows away to plant next year's crop. To miners, that first crust of ice freezing along the banks of creeks and ponds means clean-up. When freeze-up comes, it is time to stop digging and sluicing and start cleaning up the gold.

> *Winter is a necessary part of life. You can't get away from it, so you have to learn to live with it. That's when we learned a lot of things about Native life. Then in the summer, you live the things you learned. Wintertime makes you a better person, or a better hard-to-get-along-with person. To me, winter was put in the seasons to shape men's frame of mind and souls. Winter wasn't put there to be against us. It was put there to help us.*
>
> *Eskimo Woman of the Kuskokwim River Delta*

Not only the quantity of light and its cycles affect Alaskan life. The light's unique *quality* produces a heaven on earth for photographers and artists. Many compare the effect of Alaskan sunlight with the glowing illumination in paintings by Renaissance old masters. Because of the state's northern latitude, the sun is never directly overhead. With the sun at a lower angle on the horizon, its rays travel through more of the earth's atmosphere. The light is filtered and softened. Always, there are rich shadows. Winter sunsets inundate snow-covered mountainsides with hours of alpenglow—luxurious pinks cascading into royal violets.

BOUNDARIES IN THE BUSH

> *Tundra give you this calming effect... you feel like you are part of its rhythm. But the last few years now, when I go to pick berries, I see these little orange survey markers all over the tundra. They look out of place, and give you a restricted feeling. You used to be able to go anywhere with a free feeling. Now, it may be our land, but there are boundaries.*
>
> *Villager in Western Alaska*

Perhaps nowhere do the changes of the past decade and a half show up as graphically as in the Bush, in the once-isolated Native villages. Alaska's vast, roadless, rural area with its sparse, mostly Native population is called the Bush. The terms Alaska Native or Native with a capital *N* refer collectively to the land's aboriginal people—the Eskimos, Indians, and Aleuts. Non-Native people who were born in Alaska are called native Alaskans.

In the Bush, people live closer to the romantic picture of Alaska that most people have. Hunting, fishing, and trapping, rural residents follow a schedule based more on Mother Nature than on a time clock. Here, the present embodies a mixture—sometimes peaceful, sometimes violent—of past and future. Two cultures separated by generation, food, life-style, concept of time, and sometimes language live side by side.

Many villagers still rely, to a varying extent, on subsistence food-gathering from the land and waters. Native workers at Prudhoe Bay's oil fields often come home for the whale and caribou hunts. No longer dependent on spears, harpoons, or dogsleds, Native hunters rely on guns, motorboats, and snowmachines. They use CB radios to keep in touch with whaling crews in sealskin boats out in the Arctic Ocean.

Increasingly, however, the basic necessities of life—food, clothing and shelter—come not from the land, but from the store. A vast difference in perspective exists between Native people in their sixties and seventies and their grandchildren, who are growing up in a cash-based economy. An informal trade-off arrangement operates in many villages: the older people hunt and cook wild game, waterfowl, fish, and marine mammal meat and share that food with younger family members and friends. And the younger generation with jobs shares its cash with the elders.

Kotzebue Eskimo Grandmother

Besides the continuing changeover to cash, people in the Bush are experiencing other significant shifts in life-style. Attending grades seven through twelve in their own villages or nearby larger communities has made a major difference to Native young people. From territorial days until the mid-1970s, teenagers from the Bush had to leave home and family and sometimes even Alaska to receive their education. Today, in the Bush, local high schools include classes in native language, crafts, and culture along with the three R's. As with many developments, Native people see local schools as a mixed blessing. While they recognize the positive aspect of keeping families together, some parents worry that the small size of many high schools precludes the broad curriculum young people need.

Rural Alaskans have grown healthier through the 1970s and early 1980s. Contagious diseases and problems related to poor nutrition, which have plagued Native people since their first contact with Western civilization, have lessened considerably. Nearly every village now has a health aide and clinic, equipped with radio and often satellite television communication. Native health aides act as eyes, ears, and hands for doctors in distant hospitals. Despite difficulties of climate and terrain, village sanitation and water systems are being constructed. A mental and physical health movement, begun in the late 1970s, addresses rural alcohol abuse. Many communities have taken advantage of a state law which allows residents to vote whether the importation and consumption of alcohol into their community should be allowed. Unlike Prohibition, which failed, statistics show dramatic decreases in crime and health problems in villages that have banned liquor.

At the time of statehood in 1959, one dogteam still carried mail between two villages in the Arctic. Dog mushing survives today, but as a sport only. Scheduled airlines and charter Bush planes now carry mail, people, and supplies to villages, camps, and homesteads throughout rural Alaska. In Southeast, the Alaska Marine Highway System, a state-run ferry boat service, connects formerly isolated communities to each other and Seattle.

Still, new ways and development are not always welcomed with open arms. Most Native people want to proceed more slowly than government or industry resource-development timetables. Seeing oil activity spread into their backyard, the people of Barrow formed a local government called the North Slope Borough which

operates like a county and can, of course, levy taxes. Oil companies fought incorporation, until the courts settled the issue in favor of local government. The borough's subsequent capital improvements program and services have brought schools, utilities, office buildings, fuel storage, jobs, and other quality-of-life improvements to the thirty-five hundred, mostly Native residents of the 88,280-square-mile borough.

Barrow's Inupiat Eskimos have resisted most strongly the trend toward assimilation and have fostered connections with Canadian and Greenland Eskimos through the Inuit Circumpolar Conference, which has achieved official observer status in the United Nations. While some Conference members advocate creation of a totally independent Arctic nation, many would be content with enough international political clout to slow development and protect the circumpolar region's environment.

Yu'pik Eskimo Woman with Master's Degree in Anthropology

When the glaciers of the last ice age melted, the sea rose, covering the land bridge used by the prehistoric, Asian people who first settled America. Receding ice fields also revealed passes through the mountains, and the ancestors of today's American and Mexican Indians migrated south through these passageways.

In Alaska, four main ethnic groups established territorial boundaries. The Athabaskan Indians lived throughout the vast Interior, with its grassy steppes, braided rivers, and unpredictable food supply. Tribes extended into the Copper River and Cook Inlet areas of the Southcentral region.

Their neighbors, trading partners, and frequent opponents in battle were the Eskimos. While some Eskimo people roamed inland following caribou along the North Slope, most lived on the coast and depended on marine mammals and fish. Their world ranged from Southcentral's Prince William Sound and the Western Alaska region to the harsh Arctic.

In Southeastern Alaska, the Tlingit and Haida Indians, both from the same ethnic group, were skilled warriors and traders, enjoyed an abundant food supply and developed a highly complex society. Across the Gulf of Alaska to the west, the Aleuts, expert sea-going hunters, also found food plentiful and established intricate social customs.

Most of Alaska's non-perishable supplies come from the Lower 48 by container ship or barge, such as this loaded vessel entering Womans Bay on Kodiak Island.

Their feelings about the land brought the Native people together in a struggle against infringement on their way of life — infringement which began with Vitus Bering's voyage of discovery in 1741. Bering's crew brought back to Russia the electrifying news of an incredible wealth of sea otter and other fur-bearing animals in the land which lay to the east. So the rush for Alaska's riches, which marked the end of the Natives' isolation from the Western world, began.

During the long years that they occupied Russian America, the Russians made no treaties or other land-ownership arrangements with Alaska's aboriginal people. When the United States purchased Alaska in 1867, the Americans simply guaranteed Natives their "historic rights," whatever that might mean.

The Alaska Statehood Act of 1959 entitled the state to select 103 million acres from the unappropriated majority of Alaska's land. By giving the new state title to land which contained valuable natural resources, Congress hoped the fledgling government would become economically self-sufficient. But when the state began to choose its acreage and to publicize its ambitious plans for resource development, it ran headlong into the Native people. They were filing claims to Alaska's land by right of original occupancy and use. The Secretary of the Interior appointed a mostly

Native committee to draft legislation, and in 1968 the battle moved into the halls of Congress.

Later that year, an unexpected ally of the Native people held a press conference. The oil industry announced discovery of a "supergiant" oilfield on Alaska's North Slope. A pipeline to carry the Prudhoe Bay oil to market could not be built until title to lands along the pipeline route was settled. Oil companies joined the state government and Alaska's Congressional delegation in a final push for settlement. In December, 1971, agreement came.

> *I always thought "Native" meant where I was from, not who I was . . . until Land Claims. It used to be that we had the village, our language, and subsistence life-style that held us together. Now we have our heritage and the corporation.*
>
> *Aleut Village Leader*

The Alaska Native Claims Settlement Act awarded the state's Native people nearly one billion dollars in cash and forty-four million acres of land. This settlement, unlike previous ones with American Indians, gave administrative power to the Native people themselves. Eskimos, Indians, or Aleuts who had at least one Native grandparent and had been born before December 18, 1971 were eligible for benefits under the Land Claims Settlement Act. But rather than direct payments to individuals, Congress chose that flower of twentieth century capitalism—the corporation—as the means for distribution of money and land.

Equal opportunity laws gave women and Natives the chance for lucrative trade union and management jobs during the three-year construction of the pipeline.

Twelve regional corporations, with a thirteenth one for Natives living outside Alaska, were organized with Native people as the stockowners. Within each region, Natives became shareholders in their own village corporations as well.

Many Natives did not know whether the corporation idea would work. As a Northwest Alaska village leader said, it would be a giant step for most of the Native people, many of whom still depended largely on subsistence—hunting, fishing, berrypicking —for their livelihood. Enrollment in the corporations and organizational meetings were conducted in the Eskimo languages, which have no words for corporation or stockholder. For the first five years, Natives lobbied for their rights, enrolled their people, surveyed and studied land. According to many, there was a heady feeling of finally having some control over their future.

Native corporations differ from most public corporations in that their directors are also owners, stockholders, and generally related to each other and to other stockholders. Native corporations are concerned about the social, educational, employment, and housing needs of their people. Striking a healthy balance between social action and money-making remains a difficult and sometimes emotional dilemma for many regional corporation leaders. Conscience may pull one way, while the articles of incorporation demand another emphasis. Non-profit corporations in each region have been set up to address housing, employment, and other social issues. The state contracts with many of these organizations to provide human services on the local level.

Sled dog racers breed for sprints—short day-races up to thirty miles long—and for endurance marathons like the Kuskokwim three hundred-mile race and the three to four-week Iditarod.

One of the Interior regional corporation's culturally important investments, though not a big money-maker, was underwriting *Spirit of the Wind.* A feature film on George Attla, the Huslia villager who overcame polio to be a world champion dog musher, *Spirit* gives an accurate picture of the heritage of rural Alaska, family closeness, and Native ties to the land.

> *Most Native people I know—and they're of all ages—don't really want the old ways back. It was pretty tough back then. But they want the old values.*
>
> *Southeast Non-Native Resident*

Regional "Elders Conferences" began in the early 1970s. Their purpose: to share and preserve the old ways still remembered by a mere handful of people in some areas but by nearly everyone over the age of twenty in others. The conferences are videotaped, so the wisdom and teachings of the old people will remain when they have gone. Since the early 1970s, traditional family and church influences in the Bush seem to have lessened. In 1975, rural youngsters began to discover the hypnotic appeal of the outside world via television, as state-supported satellite receiving stations in most villages brought network programming. New expectations, new demands for consumer products are the result.

Ironically, the very thing which has given Alaska's seventy-six thousand Eskimo, Indian, and Aleut people equal legal and economic stature and reawakened their pride in themselves and their heritage has also propelled them into the economic fast lane of the twentieth century. There they must stay if they are to keep the land and money they have achieved. But exploiting the land, even for their own use, carries with it an inner conflict for many leaders. The call of simpler ways brings many urban Natives back to their childhood haunts for visits. They remember summers at fish camp, with no regular schedules, only fishing and conversation to fill the long, relaxed days. They leave behind corporate offices to renew their ties with another part of themselves.

Yet it remains an open question whether corporate investments and services will stand the test of 1991, the year when Native-owned stock—and thus control of Native lands—can be sold to non-Native people. To hedge against the attraction of quick bucks from selling stock, the Native groups focus on "stockholder hire" for projects which include mining, fishing, timber development, construction, oil services, jade exporting and reindeer herding. Native corporations also have invested in hotels, office buildings, financial institutions, transportation, and communications.

The Alaska Native Land Claims Settlement also produced an unexpected effect among many non-Native Alaskans. An Anchorage attorney explains that the settlement opened people's eyes to a different way of looking at property: through the land, people are connected to the past and to inner values.

Southcentral Indian Elder

Increasing numbers of non-Native people also call the Bush home. Its freer life-style includes more inconveniences and more difficulties, but these are consciously chosen over the easier life and more hectic pace of larger communities. In 1970, Bethel, a regional center of Western Alaska, had approximately seventeen hundred people, with about ten Natives to every white person. By 1982, a population of approximately three thousand divided up 78 percent Native, 15 percent white, and 7 percent Filipino, Korean, Black, Hispanic, Vietnamese, Greek, and Latin American. The statistics are typical of larger Bush communities. Alaska has become the traditional American melting pot.

While they continue to live closer to the land, Bush residents are less and less isolated. Not only do they travel often and easily, but more and more frequently the world arrives at their doorstep. Since the early 1970s, representatives of government and private enterprise have traveled increasingly to the Bush, as have growing numbers of people heading out to enjoy Alaska's wilderness. Many larger Bush communities now have restaurants and hotels, and they welcome travelers.

Radio, both public and commercial, serves as a chief source of weather forecasts and local information, including such items as where polar bear meat is available, when a member of an isolated family is planning to catch the mail plane back home, who needs help fishing or running a trapline, and what snow machine parts have arrived at the village store. Many Bush stations broadcast in one or more Native languages as well as English.

Those rugged Alaskan folk heroes, the Bush pilots, are still alive and well, although most have updated their operations. Today, the male or female pilot flies for a professionally managed air-taxi service and uses planes which are clean, well-maintained, and equipped with the most sophisticated navigational aids and radios available. "Flying by the seat of your pants" skills certainly work in a pinch, but the emphasis — thanks to customer demand and competition — now lies on safety and professionalism.

In the 1982 statewide election, controversy arose over whether rural residents should have broader access than sports hunters and fishermen to the state's wildlife resources. The vote favored preserving subsistence rights, but the question represents, in a microcosm, Alaska's larger issue in the 1980s: to live with both frontier patterns of thinking and present-day perspectives, to live with both old and new ways.

COMMUNITY PATTERNS

Anchorage Political Leader and Business Owner

Alaskan cities offer all the features of contemporary urban living: symphony orchestras and opera companies, automatic teller machines, rush hours, high-rise hotels, European shoes, lectures and film festivals, shopping centers, fast food restaurants, daily jet service to the world, cabaret entertainment, museums, gourmet restaurants, public and private higher education.

"We enjoy the inconsistency of our modern world here," says one Kodiak writer. "The electricity frequently goes out in the winter and we have to light up the wood stove and oil lamps. Life goes on pretty much as usual, except that we can't run our word processor or video game."

At the time of statehood, Anchorage had become the state's largest city, a thriving young community of about one hundred thousand people. A quarter of a century later, Anchorage is bursting at the seams with 230,000 residents. Still full of dynamic life, it is the center of the state's transportation, communication, and business network; a powerful city surrounded by snow-capped mountains and the shining waters of Cook Inlet. It is still possible to see moose from the freeways; glass-walled office towers sit close to old log cabins; the professional Alaska Repertory Theatre draws the same large, enthusiastic group of fans as the World Championship Sled Dog Race which runs through the center of town.

Fairbanks, the "Golden Heart" of Alaska's Interior, lies along the gentle bends of the Chena River in the Tanana Valley. Originally begun as a gold mining town, the community of nearly sixty thousand began its stable, prosperous economic cycle in the mid-1970s as the supply center for pipeline construction. In the 1980s, the trend continues with new services, new highways, new homes and businesses. The University of Alaska, which began in Fairbanks as a land-grant institution in 1917, has grown to include colleges in the arts and sciences, several masters and doctoral programs, an impressive library, dormitories, and a student center. People in Fairbanks exhibit a broad range of life-styles. Some professors choose to live in log cabins without running water or electricity, while some dog mushers and miners build expensive split-level homes.

Alaska's next largest communities nestle picturesquely beneath mountains along the North Pacific. In Southeast, the state capital of Juneau ranks as the third-largest borough in the state with nearly twenty-three thousand people. On the tip of Alaska's panhandle, in fourth place, is Ketchikan with fourteen thousand. Kodiak Island in the Gulf of Alaska, home to thirteen thousand residents, is the state's fifth-largest borough; in sixth place with eight thousand is Sitka. Alaska has fewer than ten other communities with a thousand or more residents. The larger communities in Southeast and on Kodiak rely chiefly on timber and fish, which produce seasonal, cyclical economies. Juneau began and prospered with gold until the 1940s, when government took over as the stable economic influence.

A campaign to move the capital from Southeast, closer to the majority of the state's population and to a location accessible by road, resulted in a decade-long series of statewide votes. The 1982 election seemed to settle the issue, but while Alaskans approved the move, they did not approve any money to carry it out. Another effort to unify the state's widely separated regions came in 1983 when Alaska's four time zones were consolidated into two. For the first time since the 1800s, 98 percent of Alaska's residents finally operate on the same clock.

Most Alaskans point to the nearby wilderness as one of the main reasons they love Alaskan life. The boundaries of all Alaska's cities, municipalities, and boroughs contain wild, natural land. State and national parklands often lie adjacent to neighborhoods. Much of east Anchorage is also Chugach State Park, while the Chugach National Forest covers much of Southcentral Alaska. The Tongass National Forest encircles most Southeast cities, a pattern repeated throughout the state with national interest lands and communities. Moose in the cabbage patch and bears in the berry patch remind us of how truly close Alaska's wilderness is.

Anchorage Entrepreneur

Not all Alaskans, however, think the supreme value of the wilderness includes actually getting *into* it. At least, not to the extent of sleeping in a tent fifty miles from nowhere and being bitten by swarms of famished mosquitoes. Many Alaskans enjoy the scenic settings of their cities. They flightsee and relax in the domed observation cars of the Alaska Railroad. They watch huge icebergs calve off the face of tidewater glaciers as they ride aboard warm cabin cruisers or tour ships in Prince William Sound and Glacier Bay. They drive motor homes along paved highways through the Kenai National Wildlife Refuge or Denali State Park. They appreciate the wilderness for the inspiration it provides to Alaska's thriving arts community. They take pleasure in Alaska's opportunities, people, and community activities.

Alaska's system of higher education offers much to both the full-time student pursuing an academic career or to the person wanting to pick up a few useful skills. State-supported schools include the University of Alaska at Anchorage, Fairbanks, and Juneau; Anchorage Community College; and eleven other community colleges and rural extension services. At the internationally acclaimed Geophysical Institute in Fairbanks, scientists from around the world conduct research on Arctic and sub-Arctic conditions. Along with the private Alaska Pacific University in Anchorage and Sheldon Jackson College in Sitka, these schools offer a wide range of courses to more than twenty-eight thousand students. Classes with a distinctly Alaskan flavor include the Yup'ik Eskimo language, Native grass-basket weaving, log cabin building, and dog mushing.

One in forty-five Alaskans holds a pilot's license. Near Anchorage International Airport lies the world's largest floatplane base at Lakes Hood and Spenard.

The 1970s era of Native land claims, oil development, and good, steady economic conditions attracted a large number of professional people to the state — doctors, lawyers, professors, natural resource experts, engineers, business managers, and government administrators, as well as forest, fishery, construction and agriculture workers with experience in modern technology. The 1970s also brought some people who did not necessarily choose Alaska. Until then — unless you served with Uncle Sam — most non-Native residents came because they *wanted* to. With large corporations rotating employees into Alaska, and workers wanting "to make a nest egg in a few years, then get the hell out," many pre-pipeline Alaskans notice a higher level of transience in Alaskan society.

> *I find I'm not quite as willing to invest a lot of myself immediately in new people in the community as I used to be, because I'm not sure they're in it for the long haul. They might just pack up and leave in a year or two.*
>
> Valdez Homemaker and Civic Volunteer

For the most part, however, Alaskans willingly open heart and hearth to the person who wants to see their home as they see it, to know a bit of the history, to appreciate the mountains and rivers. Because so many people here come from somewhere else — over

two-thirds of Alaska's population was born in a different state or country — friends become "family" and often share closer ties than relatives.

Only recently has Alaskan society begun to show some noticeable "streaks of gray." As children growing up in Fairbanks and Anchorage, we did not see a lot of older people. The deeply lined faces of Native elders fascinated us, and we loved our grandparents and their older friends *Outside.* Alaska drew young people, young families. Few older people surrounded by generations of kin and personal history decided to pack their bags and move to Alaska, and that remains true today. Alaskans average just twenty-six years of age. But the young people who came north in the 1920s, 1930s, and 1940s now find themselves with grandkids, and these pioneers are choosing to remain here when they retire. They may travel a bit more in the winter to warmer climates, but they find they miss the excitement and energy of the Northland if they are gone for very long. Alaska's overall population has finally attained the look and feel of a balanced, complete society.

A Fairbanks community organizer described the decision by the Statehood Silver Anniversary Committee to commission a sculpture for the new downtown park. All kinds of themes were considered: a gold miner; a woodsman with rifle and traps; a Native with dogteam; a sternwheeler riverboat. What did committee members finally choose as a gift to Alaska on its twenty-fifth anniversary as a state? A statue of a family. They felt it symbolized Alaska's strength in the 1980s and Alaska's vision for the future.

RESOURCE RICHES

> *From 1979 on, three things characterize Alaska's relationship with its natural resources. First, we're gaining some control: the State and Natives are getting their land conveyed from the federal government, and other development companies are getting access to the resources.*
>
> *Second, we're maturing as a state, we're beginning to look at our resources as a whole, and we're thinking about establishing a comprehensive policy about our land.*
>
> *And third, we have a unique opportunity to do all this because of our revenue from Prudhoe Bay.*
>
> State Natural Resources Consultant

The Russians were drawn by Alaska's "soft gold," and established a lucrative fur trade. By the end of the 1700s, just fifty years after Vitus Bering's discovery of Alaska, freebooting hunters had nearly exterminated the fur seal and sea otter in the Aleutians, along with the Aleut people who had been enslaved to hunt the marine mammals. The Russians moved further east, to Kodiak, Southcentral, then Southeast to maintain their fur harvest. For six more decades, the Russian America Company held its New World colony before selling the entire land to the United States on March 30, 1867 for $7,200,000.

The American press and Congress greeted the Alaska real estate deal with something less than enthusiastic support. "Walrussia!" "Seward's Folly!" they lamented, doubting the sanity of the expansionist Secretary of State, William H. Seward, who agreed to buy "An Icebox" for nearly two cents an acre. Subsequently, the federal government largely ignored its new purchase. Then came the gold rush.

Gold-seekers began trickling into the north country in the 1840s and found the yellow metal in the Fortymile country northeast of Fairbanks and inland from Cook Inlet's Turnagain and Knik Arms. They struck it big in Juneau in 1880. In 1898, the headlines of Seattle newspapers screamed "TON OF GOLD," and the Klondike flood tide hit Canada's Yukon Territory and washed over into Alaska. After the turn of the century, miners pushed on and struck gold at nearly thirty locations from Nome to Southcentral.

Faced with reports from missionaries and others decrying an Alaska with no schools, government, or courts, the United States finally admitted some responsibility for its far-flung possession. Initially, Congress responded by passing a criminal code and other provisions. Then, in 1912, it approved full territorial status. For the first time, Alaskans began to experience some control over their own destiny. Seven years before the United States adopted the Nineteenth Amendment, the first act of Alaska's newly formed legislature gave women the vote.

The early years of the twentieth century brought the development of the rich Kennecott Copper Mine in the Wrangell Mountains. Ore was moved by rail almost two hundred miles to tidewater at Cordova. The early 1900s also marked the beginning of big-time fish harvesting in the rich coastal waters from Southeast to Bristol Bay. A million-dollar salmon cannery could pay for itself in a season, and *Outside* owners became wealthy under the weak control exercised by a far-away federal government. In 1914, work began on the federally built and owned Alaska Railroad. Construction, headquartered at a tiny settlement near the mouth of Ship Creek, kicked off a boom that mushroomed into a new city called Anchorage. Immense implications for the future occurred eight years later, in 1922, with the landing at Ketchikan of Alaska's first commercial airplane. Here, at last, was transportation equal to the challenge of Alaska's vast lands, mile-wide river barriers, and towering mountain ramparts.

In 1935, Alaska made headlines across the country as the site of a bold social and agricultural experiment. More than two hundred farm families from the Midwest's dustbowl relocated with federal assistance to the fertile Matanuska Valley north of Anchorage. Today, eighty pound cabbages at the State Fair bear witness to the tenacity of these "colonists" and Alaska's agricultural potential.

If "strategic location" can be called a natural resource, Alaska received high priority for development when World War II broke out. The United States military invested nearly a billion dollars in Alaska during the war years. Americans in uniform punched through the Alaska-Canada (or Alcan) Highway, now known as the Alaska Highway, at last connecting the United States by road to its northern territory. They built other roads, airfields, and installations and fought off a Japanese invasion of the Aleutian Islands, the only American soil occupied by Axis powers. Today, military men and women still comprise a significant portion of the population of Alaska — American land which at its closest point lies just three and a half miles from Russia.

By the war's end, Alaska's population ballooned from seventy-four thousand in 1941 to over one hundred and twenty thousand. Drillers found oil on the Kenai Peninsula, commercial fishing continued to prosper, and the United States Forest Service opened some of its vast timberlands in Southeast and Southcentral to harvesting. In the following years, Alaskans wanted more local control of their resources, wealth, and society. They wanted statehood. Just as the country had been reluctant in accepting its new purchase a century before, Congress was slow to make Alaska a full-fledged partner in the Union. Finally, statehood became official January 3, 1959. With high hopes, Alaskans began their modern era as residents of the 49th State.

From statehood on, Alaska's story of natural resource development can be explained almost entirely by one word: oil. Alaska's first governor, William Egan, encouraged oil exploration by making state land accessible to oil company geologists. With producing oil wells on the Kenai Peninsula, the young industry was off to a respectable start. Ten years later, eight thousand feet down under Alaska's remote North Slope, oil men found the big one: the Prudhoe Bay field.

PIPELINE TIMES

Alaska's North Slope had oil. But how to get it out and not disrupt the caribou migration or ruin the environment in the process? For nearly five years following Atlantic Richfield's discovery of a "supergiant" oilfield on the North Slope, awesome challenges faced Alyeska Pipeline Service Company, the consortium of eight oil companies formed to build the largest private construction project in history. The task: to design an 800-mile pipeline that would carry crude oil safely over Arctic tundra and permafrost, three mountain ranges, major earthquake fault zones, and hundreds of rivers and streams to tankers waiting at the ice-free port of Valdez. The pipeline was not only the largest private project in history. At a cost of $8 billion, it also became the most expensive, and from an environmental standpoint, the most closely scrutinized.

Awesome wild landscape, wind that never stops, bizarre artificial lights illuminating the camp and construction in winter. It's an experience I'll never forget: the constant drone of equipment, the potpourri of people, the strange society of mostly men, few women, no kids or elderly folks or pets. Bears in camp…drugs, food … long hours, good pay. The whole experience and life-style made even more of an impression on me than the construction work itself.

Former Member, Teamsters Union

In 1974, the United States Senate approved the Alaska Pipeline Authorization Act. Less than a year later, I answered the siren call of big bucks and adventure. Following in the footsteps of my grandfather, who ninety years before had headed north in the Klondike and Alaskan stampedes, I quit my professional job, signed up with a trade union, and became one of the twenty-two thousand people working on the pipeline. This was our gold rush.

Pipeliners formed a fluid work force. Our number at any one time varied by several thousand depending on the season and building timetable. By the end of the three-year construction phase, the project had employed more than seventy thousand people: young and mature, seasoned and green, educated and unschooled, Americans and foreigners, dedicated workers and adventurers. Just as "stockholder hire" is a priority for the Native corporations, "Alaska hire" had political power during pipeline construction, and many Alaskans jumped at the never-before-seen chance for jobs like these. On the trans-Alaska pipeline, women and Natives received their first real taste of construction work, which gave them experience and financial resources.

The wages? High. Work schedules? Typically, nine weeks on, two off; seven twelves (seven days a week, twelve hours a day) plus overtime. Camp food? Rivaled or bettered gourmet cooking in the country's finest restaurants. Room and board came free with the job if you lived in one of the twenty-nine construction camps from Prudhoe to Valdez. North of the Yukon River, along the ten-mile-wide pipeline corridor, from Coldfoot Camp to Prudhoe Bay, workers saw only other workers. From the Yukon south, "camp followers" ranging from workers' families to con artists lived in nearby communities and campgrounds.

Along with hopeful pipeliners came — of course — those with big plans to get their pay the "easier" way through gambling, drugs, prostitution, get-richer-quick schemes of every imaginable design. With Alaska's pipeline boomtown stretching from Valdez to Fairbanks, this nefarious element thrived.

A special camaraderie developed among pipeline workers who shared the experiences of adventure, accomplishment, and hardship, with hardship becoming part of the accomplishment and adventure. Nothing quite duplicates the experience of pulling on three layers of inner clothing, three pairs of socks inside felt liners and boots, down jacket, insulated coveralls, two layers of gloves, a hat, hardhat, arctic parka, and face scarf — and going out to fuel equipment, which had to run constantly in the dry, minus fifty degree temperatures. Workers on the southern part of the line faced different challenges: Valdez receives more than sixty inches of rain and more than three hundred inches of snow each year. In fact, a twenty-four hour snowfall dropping three feet of the wet, heavy white stuff is not unusual.

Wildlife abounded along the pipeline route. Around the construction prowled bears, wolves, and foxes interested in the easy and artificial food source of camp dumps and illegal handouts. Workers whose jobs took them out along the line would see brown and black bears, moose, Dall sheep, caribou, foxes, wolves, eagles, and waterfowl. Ravens were everywhere.

Studies completed at the end of construction and since then show that development through Alaska's wilderness and on the

North Slope has somewhat affected the natural patterns of animals, fish, and waterfowl. However, as one biologist noted, "Some of these effects aren't necessarily bad or good. Whenever you introduce modern society into a wilderness environment, the animals make changes and adjustments." An example is the caribou herd in the central Arctic, whose traditional calving ground includes the Prudhoe Bay area. The herd population has been growing by up to 13 percent a year since the studies began in the mid-1970s. Although caribou bulls are often seen around the rigs and roads, the cows have moved to the east and west of oil field activity to give birth, as with their calves they tend to avoid people. Despite on-going environmental impact studies, no one knows what will happen now that expanding exploration and development are moving increasingly into those areas as well.

The tiny forget-me-not, Alaska's state flower, decorates alpine meadows and streambeds from Southeast to the Arctic and even the Aleutian Islands.

State and federal agencies monitored the environmental effects of construction, and the government has funded subsequent studies, primarily north of the Brooks Range, on caribou, waterfowl, fish, and to some extent on bears. Realizing the critical importance of additional data, the oil companies have continued to conduct extensive ecological surveys of the North Slope, the pipeline corridor, and the Port of Valdez where tankers take on Alaskan oil. The results of this research point to a relatively minimal effect overall on fish and wildlife species. While many questions remain about the long-term impact of development on Alaska's flora and fauna, preserving the state's unique wilderness character remains a vital concern to those involved in the Alaska of today — and tomorrow.

Experts from all over the world come to study the pipeline as a marvel of engineering accomplishment. Insulated to hold in the oil's original heat, Prudhoe crude comes out of the ground at an average of 160 degrees Fahrenheit. Over four hundred miles of the forty-eight-inch diameter pipe lies on above-ground supports where permafrost underlies the thin layer of vegetation. The rest of the line is buried. The job of monitoring the oil flow falls to people in control rooms at both ends of the line and in ten pump stations which are equipped with millions of dollars worth of electronic equipment and computers. Even before construction could begin, the oil company consortium had to bridge the Yukon River and construct a 380-mile road north to Prudhoe Bay. Known during construction as the North Slope Haul Road, the all-gravel Dalton Highway opened to the public as far north as the Brooks Range in 1981.

As construction neared completion in May, 1977, the stampede feeling ebbed. June 20 marked "oil-in," when the first oil was pumped into the new pipeline at Prudhoe Bay for its week-long journey to the line's southern end. Since then, "Happily for us, there's been nothing but boring, monotonous, near flawless operation," remarked the operator at Prudhoe Bay's Operations Control Center. Daily, the line brings 1.7 million barrels of oil to Valdez, where it is carried by supertanker to United States refineries. Alaskan petroleum supplies about one-seventh of the United States' demand for crude oil.

A WORLD MARKETPLACE

Former Alaska Governor

Thanks to revenues from the oil industry, the state treasury mushroomed from several million dollars in 1968 to more than a billion dollars in 1982. Suddenly, Alaska found itself in the somewhat embarrassing position of having surplus money in a time when the rest of the country felt the effects of economic recession.

Yet Alaska faces needs long ago met in other states. In transportation, communication, utilities, and public facilities, it lags decades behind the norm *Outside*. Following a precedent established by oil-rich Alberta, Canada, Alaska set aside a portion of its oil revenues in a Permanent Fund designed to finance projects which will benefit future generations. To benefit the present generation, the legislature voted to distribute $1,000 checks from the Fund's earnings to every Alaskan resident in 1982. The remainder of the money flows to local and regional projects and to state government.

In a way, the pipeline symbolizes a whole new era: an opening up of the state, its land, society, and resources. When most Alaskans talk about "The Pipeline," they think of a myriad of changes which happened because of or along with the pipeline from 1974 to mid-1977. The pipeline opened the last wilderness expanse with a road to the Arctic Ocean. It opened America's eyes and consciousness in a new way to Alaska's rich storehouse of natural resources, which range from non-renewable to renewable, from oil and minerals to wilderness and wildlife.

Even as oil wealth flowed into the state's coffers, business and political leaders began planning the development of Alaska's other resources, which will play an increasingly important role in Alaska's economy when petroleum production from Prudhoe Bay begins to decline in the 1990s. Unless new fields are discovered in other areas of the state and beneath its extensive Outer Continental Shelf, Alaskans will again find themselves dependent on other resources for income and jobs.

Anchorage Resources Lawyer

While little of Alaska's immense natural gas reserves were tapped by the early 1980s, some liquified natural gas began to be shipped from Southcentral Alaska via tanker to Asia. More development plans for the state's gas, including a possible pipeline to the Lower 48, are on the drawing boards. Meanwhile, Koreans are also interested in Alaska's coal. Alaska has thousands of billions of tons of coal: more than enough to meet every projected energy need in the state for centuries. Compared to cleaner fuels such as oil and gas, coal ranks low on America's list of attractive energy sources. Asian countries have diversified their energy sources and may prove willing coal customers for years to come. A planned lead and zinc mine on the Seward Peninsula and a Southeastern site rich in molybdenum (which is used to strengthen steel) may be the first of Alaska's hard-rock minerals to receive serious consideration soon. Other areas of the state also show tremendous potential for mineral reserves.

But oil, especially the free-flowing abundance of it, has made it difficult for Alaskans to get excited about developing other mineral resources which may take more work. "We've gotten used to prosperity without hustle," remarked one state economic development expert. At the same time, Alaska's lack of infrastructure—networks of transportation and communication hamper full-scale development of most resources, which lie in out-of-the-way locations. Rural Alaska is an expensive place to do business, mainly because major support systems must be constructed before any work can begin. The largely automated oil and gas industries require a relatively small work force, thus largely avoiding the high cost of labor in Alaska. Mining and other labor-intensive industries may have to wait for world demand to rise and for new technology to make them economically viable in Alaska.

Early prosperity marked the logging industry in Southeast, where more than ninety percent of Alaska's forest products, produced in Japanese-owned pulp and lumber mills, go to Japan. Following nearly a decade-long slump, harvesting and mill operations began gearing up in 1983, and several Native corporations are beginning joint-venture harvests of their rich timber lands with domestic and foreign partners.

Since agriculture in Alaska first began, farmers have faced high costs and the question, "Where do we sell what we grow?" Agricultural potential is certainly high: the long daylight hours of Alaska's relatively short summers produce huge vegetables and grains of extremely high protein content. Furthermore, extensive grasslands make fine rangelands. Again, Alaskans look with high hopes to Asia as a potentially large, long-term market.

With more miles of coastline and continental shelf than all the rest of the United States put together, Alaska has long appreciated its immense fisheries resource. Successful seasons, however, alternate with disastrous ones, depending on the cycles of different runs and species. The 200-mile limit, established in 1978, marked a new era of development for the industry, whose historical mainstay has been salmon. Interest has turned to bottom fish, a resource long used by the Asians and Russians, and sustained yield harvesting has been emphasized.

Scientists still have much to learn about the marine food chain, as evidenced by the puzzling king crab cycle. The Aleutians' king crab fishery propelled the port of Unalaska into the number one slot in the United States in terms of overall fishing income, and the boom continued through the 1981 season. In 1982, the fishery collapsed, resulting in an early closing by Alaska Department of Fish and Game officials, and the season did not open in 1983.

Research on the fisheries is underway, along with hatchery construction, restocking, and increased harvesting of non-traditional products, such as kelp and sea urchins, which are in great demand in Asia. As with other natural resources, Native corporations are involved, joint-venturing both small and large fishing and processing operations.

Alaska's visitors are often referred to as a renewable resource, and tourism vies with fishing for second place in producing income and jobs. American and international travelers are drawn to the mystique of the "Alaskan Experience." The appeal combines romance, extraordinary environmental extremes, and exotic wilderness: the splendor so dear to every Alaskan.

As early as the 1800s, Alaska had visitors. For many years, Sitka, the capital of Russian America, was known as the "Paris of the Pacific" to European and Asian explorers, merchants, and sailors. The Inside Passage through Southeastern became popular by 1900, and Alaska's other waterways and overland routes took hardy travelers through the Interior up into the Arctic. By the 1950s, the number of visitors increased dramatically as airplanes and roads provided easier access to more regions of the state.

Like Alaska's other resources, tourism requires support services. This means everything from access to accommodations.

Alaska's land, which faces increasing use from both residents and visitors, needs careful management. Ways must be developed for people to enjoy the wilderness while making the minimum possible impact on the natural environment.

OUR WILD LAND

Robert Service
Spell of the Yukon

What magnificent land it is! From the sky-piercing, sheer rock spires of the Arrigetch Peaks in the Gates of the Arctic National Park and Preserve to the vast floodplain of the Yukon Flats National Wildlife Refuge; from the one hundred-degree summer highs of Kobuk Valley National Park's desert sand dunes to the minus seventy-degree winter lows of the Tetlin National Wildlife Refuge; from the largest sanctuary for brown bears in the United States at Katmai National Park and Preserve to the world's greatest nesting population of bald eagles in Admiralty Island National Monument — here is Alaska's wild land.

From the tip of Southeast all around the coastline to Alaska's northwest corner stretches a mind-boggling potpourri of more than twenty-four hundred islands, reefs, headlands, rocks, and spires which constitute the Alaska Maritime National Wildlife Refuge. Home to more than twenty million seabirds—about two-thirds of Alaska's total — the refuge contains the largest marine bird population in the Northern Hemisphere. Misty Fiords National Monument, which lies in Southeast, encompasses cloud-shrouded cliffs higher than those in Yosemite Valley, blue green waterways, dense rain forest, cascading waterfalls, wild rivers, and clear alpine lakes.

One of the world's largest volcanic craters forms the phenomenal six-mile-wide centerpiece of the remote and inhospitable Aniakchak National Monument, Preserve and Wild River. Nearby on the Alaska Peninsula, the Katmai National Park and Preserve includes a desolate moonscape left by the 1912 lava flow which buried a twenty-mile long valley under pumice and ash. This Valley of Ten Thousand Smokes area so approximates what space scientists expected to find on the moon that they sent the astronauts there with their special lunar vehicle to test its performance.

In northwestern Alaska, nearly the entire watershed of the Noatak River, which accommodates 350-mile-long float trips, is designated as wilderness in the Noatak National Preserve. On the opposite side of the state, more than three-fourths of the 12.4 million-acre Wrangell-Saint Elias National Park and Preserve carry the wilderness designation. Adjoining Canada's Kluane National Park, the rugged, glaciated Wrangell-Saint Elias area contains some of North America's highest peaks, including 18,008-foot Mount Saint Elias as well as the massive Bagley Icefield, which measures 190 miles long and 4,000 feet thick. Its vast Malaspina Glacier is one and a half times the size of the state of Delaware. Together, the Wrangell-Saint Elias and Kluane parks have been designated a World Heritage Site.

The 114 beach-sand ridges of Cape Krustenstern National Monument contain artifacts from every known Eskimo occupation of North America since 6000 B.C., while the Bering Land Bridge National Preserve was established primarily to protect the resources used by local Native people for their subsistence lifestyle. Several other parklands preserve areas important in Alaska's history: Baranof Castle Hill and Old Sitka State Historic Sites commemorate the Russian period; Totem Bight State Historic Park features nineteenth century totem poles carved by Tlingit and Haida Indians; Iditarod National Historical Trail, Klondike Gold Rush National Historical Park, and Independence Mine State Historic Park honor Alaska's gold mining past; Fort Abercrombie State Historic Park memorializes World War II; and the Trans-Alaska Pipeline Utility Corridor marks the transportation pathway for the state's "black gold," oil.

No list of Alaska's parklands would be complete without mention of the two most popular: Glacier Bay and Denali. In the 1790s, Captain George Vancouver sailed through Southeast mapping and naming geographic features. He scarcely noted Glacier Bay because it existed only as a slight indentation in an icefield several miles thick which almost filled the Bay to its headlands. Now, two centuries later, the glacial rivers have retreated, exposing numerous inlets in a bay up to sixty-five miles long. Spilling down between lofty mountains, sixteen sapphire blue tidewater glaciers plunge into equally azure, ice-choked fjords rimmed by tide-scoured beaches protected as Glacier Bay National Park and Preserve. Icy, plankton-filled waters sustain whales, porpoises, sea lions, and seals, while the thick coastal forest supports a healthy wildlife population.

The Athabaskan Indians called it Denali, "the high one", and the name now refers to the great Interior conservation area formerly known as Mount McKinley National Park. Expanded and renamed in 1980, the six million-acre Denali National Park and Preserve straddles an awesome 160-mile section of the Alaska range, containing, of course, Mount McKinley, locally referred to as Denali, and Mount Foraker, originally called Menlale or Denali's wife, which at 17,395 feet is barely three thousand feet shorter. Along with "The Mountain" itself and an extensive glacial system, this most-visited of Alaska's parks presents an abundant and visible spectrum of Alaska wildlife. Thirty-seven species range across rolling, open tundra.

Skagway burst into life with the great 1898 Klondike gold rush, commemorated today in the Trail of '98 Museum, located in City Hall. Nearby is the famous Chilkoot Pass.

The Alaska Native Claims Settlement Act did more than just set aside Alaska's land heritage for Native people. It also laid the groundwork for legislation that would preserve for all Americans part of the still untouched natural wilderness abundant in Alaska. Unlike most areas in the Lower 48, Alaska's territory was held by the Federal government in the unappropriated public domain since it was acquired from Russia.

At the turn of the century, President Theodore Roosevelt designated 24 million acres of the highest quality timberland in Alaska as the Chugach and Tongass National Forests. Over the following decades, additional designations for specific purposes amounted to one-fourth of Alaska's 375 million acres. By statehood in 1959, less than *2 percent* of Alaska's land was in private hands. Thus, the state had considerable real estate from which to choose its 103 million acres, as did the Native people in selecting their 44 million acres.

The Native land settlement rode in on a perfectly timed crest of public opinion. Conservationists around the country caught hold of the same wave. They supported the Natives' bill, because it also promised to put environmental concerns into law. Section 17(d)(2) of the Alaska Native Claims Settlement Act called for the Secretary of the Interior to set aside Alaska's most unique and spectacular land in the "national interest".

Following passage of the Act, all interested parties began intensive surveys and land and resource studies. Just as the time limit set by the Act for specific designations was about to expire in 1979, Secretary of the Interior Cecil Andrus withdrew over one-third of the state's acreage for parklands. Across Alaska, a howl of protest erupted. Many residents, threatened with loss of public land, which they used for their livelihoods or simply enjoyed, agreed with the opinion of one angry hunting guide in the Wrangell Mountains: "Those Outsiders ruined all their land so now they're telling us what to do with ours!" Or, as a state biologist put it, "It's hard to accept the end of the American dream: endless land, free for the staking."

I think we really wanted the same thing in the end: land that remained natural and free. But passions got so high. Conservationists thought all Alaskans were poised at the edge of our forests with bulldozers, and we thought they wanted everything for a park no one could even walk in. Plus, Alaskans have a history of being controlled by far-away interests who don't understand our special conditions and life-styles. For a while, "WE DON'T GIVE A DAMN HOW THEY DO IT OUTSIDE" was the most popular bumper sticker in the state. Alaskans were used to thinking of the wilderness in terms of our "rights:" to use for hunting and fishing, mining, exploring, building a cabin. It's tough to accept that this isn't really our land, but wilderness that belongs to the whole country.

Fairbanks Lands Attorney

Within our parklands lies the Alaska of our hearts. Most Alaskans want their children to know wilderness so wild it puts them in touch with a different time and rhythm and with the simplicity that north country poet Robert Service captures:

The strong life that never knows harness;
The wilds where the caribou call;
The freshness, the freedom, the farness—
O God! How I'm stuck on it all.

On December 2, 1980, a stroke of President Jimmy Carter's pen designated a total of approximately 104 million acres of Alaska, an area larger than California, as National Parks, National Forests, Wild and Scenic Rivers, and National Wildlife Refuges. (The exact acreage is constantly changing as lands are surveyed, boundaries stabilized, and state and private lands transferred.)

The Alaska National Interest Lands Conservation Act, or "d-2 legislation", approached land classification in a more holistic

Supported by state funding and encouraged by an Asian market, farmers in Big Delta, one hundred miles southeast of Fairbanks, clear land to raise barley and other grains.

manner than had been done generally in the country's past. First, efforts were made to protect entire ecosystems, whether by adding land to existing areas or by creating completely new conservation units. For instance, in the Brooks Range, continuous wildlife habitat lies safely within protected boundaries, thus pre-

With nearly 340,000 volumes, Anchorage's University of Alaska Library also serves the adjoining campuses of Anchorage Community College and Alaska Pacific University.

serving most of the migration route of the Porcupine (River) caribou herd. Second, traditional subsistence hunting, fishing, and trapping by rural people are allowed inside newly created national parks and wildlife refuges. Third, planes, powerboats, and snowmobiles may be used for access into wilderness areas. Provisions were also made for retaining, maintaining, and building shelter cabins for public safety. Fourth, recognizing Alaska's immense oil, gas, and mineral potential, many areas were excluded from wilderness classification to allow development.

When all the protected federal lands—approximately 152.2 million acres—are added to the state government's more than 3.5 million acres, Alaska's parklands cover an area just slightly smaller than the state of Texas and larger than the combined states of California, Pennsylvania, and Indiana.

Each of the two state and four federal agencies responsible for managing the different conservation lands has different goals and objectives, ranging from multiple use to wilderness preservation. Many politicians, land users, and conservationists continue to strive for additional changes in the status of Alaska's lands— ranging from more land for hunting to more protection of wilderness. Alaskans face a great challenge to move away from a pioneer "tame the land" attitude and become more comfortable with their role as stewards of a last great frontier.

VIEWS, VISIONS, AND MAGIC

I think what makes Alaskan society so unique is the broad range of what we accept as "normal." Whaling from a skin boat seems normal. Sitting in a private club twenty stories above Anchorage, cutting a multi-million dollar real estate deal seems normal. Furthermore, the same person might be doing both. And there's a whole lot of living in between those two extremes that's just as "Alaskan."
Kenai Peninsula Banker

Alaska seems to draw a certain type of person: one who is willing to take risks and create a new life away from the comfortable patterns and associations of established America. One with a zest for living!

One thing Alaskans have always been is outspoken. Many personally know their elected representatives and most have definite opinions about public policy. There is a general consensus that the views of residents count and that individuals have the power to influence the system. T-shirts advertising a musical written by a former Juneau resident referred to "ALASKA—LAND OF THE INDIVIDUAL AND OTHER ENDANGERED SPECIES." More Alaskans register "Independent" than for Republican and Democratic parties combined. Because of the state's small population, every vote, every voice at public hearings matters. Divergent views forecast the future. Certain Alaskans espouse a proud, booster approach which sees government existing to promote business interests, growth, and development. Many of these people remember an Alaska that needed everything: airports, schools, roads, telephones, stores. They have helped to build the Alaska of today.

Other equally dedicated Alaskans head toward a different goal. In their opinion, Alaska may not have moved slowly enough through the seventies, despite the best efforts of the "limited growth" state administration. Mineral deposits are now being developed in wildlife and waterfowl habitat areas. New roads and mining are affecting salmon spawning streams, and oil exploration is occurring in Arctic waters. These residents believe more research is necessary and that in Alaska is a precious last chance to preserve the wild heritage of America.

Some say hunting in national parks must be allowed because Alaskans have hunted in these lands traditionally. Others say that the days are well past when Alaska did not need wilderness trails, campgrounds, and privvies. It used to be that a person could take an axe anywhere, cut tent poles, rig a camp, and burn wood. Alaska is big, conservationists agree, but they caution that if we are not careful, we will be finding trash in places we cannot believe people have ever been. The challenge is to both use and protect the land.

Alaska's smaller population means everyone has opportunities to do more things, whether that means participating in civic organizations or serving on public boards and commissions. Many businesses are started because no one in town yet offers that service or product. "Where else would 'hunting and fishing' qualify as acceptable experience for the job of president of a multi-million dollar corporation?" asks a Native regional corporation executive.

A feeling of freedom to try anything you want permeates the state. What is more, most people leap at the chance to support new ideas. Want to build a log cabin in the woods? The brother of your college roommate advises that a man over in Manley Hot Springs does excellent work. "Just call him and tell him I sent you." Want to run the Iditarod, the 1,049-mile sled dog race from Anchorage to Nome, but you have never mushed dogs before? A good friend of your Anchorage co-worker hears about your interest, and responds, "Hey, that's great! My friend in Knik will lease

Ancient subsistence life-styles mix with Western ideas. Here at the Arctic Slope Regional Corporation and Stuaqpak Store, Inupiat Eskimos take advantage of Barrow's local bus service.

you a team and teach you how to train." Want to try trapping? Your racketball partner has relatives in the Interior and quickly suggests, "My brother in Ruby runs a trap line and would like some help this winter."

Perhaps because Alaskans are still few in number and mobile in both work and recreation, they are avid "networkers." Newcomers and visitors rapidly realize it is difficult to say something in one community without its preceding them to the next. "Everybody here knows everyone else — from Ketchikan to Barrow!" a national television news producer declared in astonishment. Most Alaskans appreciate and promote the feeling of "connectedness," and freely recommend people to travelers who will be stopping in this village or that town.

Because most Alaskans have seen their own attitudes change the longer they live in the state, they tend to be patient while newcomers adjust. As a Bristol Bay pilot explains, "When people first come north, they tend to think they have all the answers. But the longer they stay in the state, the more they find new ways to look at things and they tend to drop their preconceptions and prejudgments. Maybe it's something about the vastness and diversity of the land itself that calls for an increased tolerance of people and cultures."

"If a person is willing to learn and work hard," says a Wrangell boat builder and fisherman, "Alaska offers literally anything. In fact, I find that I tend to make my choice of employees more on their willingness to take risks and enjoy new adventures than college degrees and a 'plannned career path'."

> *I don't think Alaskans are truly different from
> other people. I just think Alaska's free and plenti-
> ful opportunities allow us to come maybe a little
> closer to our individual and collective God-given
> potential.*
>
> Alaskan Broadcasting Pioneer

Many Alaskans shake their heads in sheer amazement at the headlong pace of change since 1970. While they love the vigorous, stimulating atmosphere of growth and enjoy many modern benefits, they sometimes fear Alaska is fast becoming homogenized. They worry that Alaska may be losing that specialness it has in their minds.

People who have just moved north and people who visit see Alaska through newer, fresher eyes. They see what is here, rather than what has changed. To these cheechakoes, these tourists, we ask, "Why did you come? What do you find? How do you feel about life here?"

We hear them describe a certain grandeur, magic, energy and freedom, challenge and opportunity. They remark on the cycles of midnight sun and darkness and the impact of summer and winter on activities and emotions. They marvel at the living, shifting hues of the Northern Lights. They thrill to the vibrant orange of sunrise and find themselves quiet and pensive in the purple sunset's glow. They talk about the unusual sunshine that imparts a rich, yet somehow ethereal essence to the land. "It is as though Nature thoughtfully designed Alaska's soft lighting as a perfect counterpoint to the overwhelming majesty of the land," mused one.

We know that light. And that vitality and magnetism. The Alaska they describe is the Alaska that lured men and women north to the goldfields at the turn of the century and others north in the 1940s to make a home. We hear the words that describe the Alaska we know, and we are reassured.

Right: The tall spruce and hemlock of Mitkof Island's verdant Southeast rainforest give way to meadows and muskegs. Blue grouse often inhabit the edges of these muskegs where thorny devil's club may grow twelve feet high, and the odor of pungent skunk cabbage mingles with the dank scent of the acidic bog.

Left: Salvaged from isolated locations around Southeast, nineteenth century Tlingit and Haida totems border pathways around the ceremonial clan house in Totem Bight State Historic Park. *Above:* Mother and pup harbor seals *(Phoca vitulina)* bask on an iceberg in Glacier Bay's Muir Inlet, named for famed naturalist John Muir, who first explored and documented the region in 1879. *Overleaf:* Glacier Bay barely appears on explorer George Vancouver's charts, because in 1794 it was only a slight indentation in an immense river of ice. Since then, retreating ice has left a fjord sixty-five miles long. Riggs, shown here, is one of the Bay's sixteen active, tidewater glaciers.

Southeast

Above: Gravina Island's forested peak looms out of the fog-shrouded Tongass Narrows. Ships plying the Inside Passage of Alaska's Panhandle snake their way through a misty kaleidoscope of islands and waterways. *Right:* The boundaries of the Tongass, the nation's largest national forest, encompass nearly all of Southeast, which exports timber products primarily to Japan. Boomed logs await transformation into wood chips at a sawmill on Wrangell Island. *Overleaf:* Silent storytellers of Indian history and legend, totem poles carved of the easily worked red cedar highlight the Sitka National Historical Park.

THUNDER BAY

Left: Bush planes, charter boats, and tour vessels transport adventurers into Alaska's remote regions. Hikers and kayakers bound for wilderness experiences inside Glacier Bay catch a ride aboard the *MV Thunder Bay. Above:* Icy, nutrient-rich waters near glaciers nourish tiny plankton, the lowest rung on the food chain which includes the Dungeness crab, a favorite among diners throughout the world. *Overleaf:* Planes departing Juneau's busy airport parallel Gastineau Channel. Beyond is the mile-wide base of Mendenhall Glacier, which flows down from the 1,215-square mile Juneau Icefield.

Above: A reminder of Old World heritage, traditional Norwegian tole painting decorates some of Petersburg's homes and businesses. Many residents celebrate the "Little Norway Festival" every May with dancing, costumes, Viking ships, and Scandinavian food. *Right:* Lush vegetation thrives in the warm, wet summers and mild, wet winters of the Gulf of Alaska coast. State and federal agencies try to balance preservation of critical wildlife habitats, including old-growth forests and salmon-spawning streams, with commercial logging and mining.

Left: The Tlingit Indians of Admiralty Island's Angoon village revered nearby Kootznahoo Inlet and adopted its name for their village corporation. Local and regional Native corporations throughout the state administer money and land awarded to Alaska's seventy-six thousand Eskimos, Indians, and Aleuts by the 1971 Alaska Native Claims Settlement Act. *Above:* Winter surf crashes over coastal rocks along Favorite Channel near Amalga Harbor. Juneau's North Glacier Highway ends forty-one miles up Lynn Canal. Mountains and glaciers make the state capital accessible only by plane or ship.

Haines, population fifteen hundred, boasts a mild climate which sustains Alaska's only abundant supply of apple and cherry trees. Residents honor their plum-sized strawberries with a festival each fall. Located at the northern terminus of the Inside Passage, Haines, known to the Tlingits as "Dtehshuh" or "end of the trail," and nearby Skagway are the only two cities in Southeast linked to Alaska's contiguous road system.

Above: The *MV Columbia,* 418-foot flagship of the Marine Highway System, and its sister ships provide regularly scheduled service between fourteen Southeastern ports and the Lower 48 via Prince Rupert, British Columbia, and Seattle. Another section of the System links thirteen ports in Southwestern Alaska. *Overleaf:* The *MV Taku* navigates slowly through the Wrangell Narrows during low tide, passing private fishing and pleasure boats moored at Papkes Landing. Although lacking the luxurious amenities of cruise ships, most Alaskan state ferries have staterooms, galleys, lounges, solariums, and observation rooms. United States Forest Service personnel offer summer lectures. The System provides vital, year-round transportation for residents and visitors.

Above: The sun makes such rare and welcome appearances in Southeast that territorial government workers were once given time-off during cloudless weather. Present-day ferry travelers aboard the *MV Matanuska* actively enjoy just such a holiday in Stephens Passage. *Right:* Sitka earned the nickname "Paris of the Pacific" for its lively cultural and social life in the early 1800s when it served as the capital of Russian America. After local Tlingit Indians destroyed the fledgling town, the Russians rebuilt it in 1804, fortifying the area with blockhouses and cannon. *Overleaf:* The lack of flat land around Ketchikan prompted these Ward Cove residents to build floathouses, which rest on mud flats at low tide.

Left: Saffron pond lilies brighten the dark pockets of water in muskeg bogs, which are prevalent in the coastal region's lichen-laden forests. *Above:* A strenuous climb up steep Mount Roberts yields a summer panorama of Douglas Island, Juneau, and Gastineau Channel, a narrow waterway frequented by cruise ships, ferries, float planes, fishing vessels, and pleasure boats. *Overleaf:* October through January, a late-season chum salmon run draws three thousand bald eagles — the world's largest known congregation — to a section of the Chilkat River known locally as the Chilkat Bald Eagle Council Grounds.

Above: In the 1930s, federally relocated farmers fleeing the Midwest's Dust Bowl colonized Southcentral's Matanuska Valley north of Anchorage. The short growing season's long daylight hours produce eighty-pound cabbages and other gigantic vegetables, which are spotlighted each fall at the Alaska State Fair. *Right:* With more shoreline than all the rest of the United States put together, Alaska hosts a varied abundance of coastal marine life. Prince William Sound's colorful seaweed, sea stars, and jellyfish fascinate tide-pool gazers and scuba divers.

Southcentral

Left: Alaska's profuse fireweed functions as nature's summer clock: in spring, blossoms appear at the flower's base, then bloom their way up the stalk through summer. These early August sentinels by Upper Trail Lake will last another month before their blooms dissolve into wind-blown, seed-filled cotton. *Above:* With a name befitting its majestic setting in the Wrangell Mountains, Regal Mountain towers near the once bustling mining towns of Kennecott and McCarthy. Beginning in the early 1900s, a private railroad transported millions of dollars worth of copper ore 112 miles to tidewater at Cordova, before the mine shut down in 1938.

Lords of all they survey, coastal brown
(grizzly) bears feast on salmon spawning in
the Naknek River in Katmai National Park,
the nation's largest sanctuary for these
omnivores. The average size for an adult
male ranges from 500 to 900 pounds,
though exceptionally large individuals have
been recorded at 1,400 pounds.

Above: Two residents of Kodiak, home to thirteen thousand people, stroll along Ugak Bay, a small section of the mountainous island's eight hundred-mile coastline. *Overleaf:* In January, mid-afternoon sunset glows on 6,050-foot Mount Carpathian, which overlooks Turnagain Arm near Portage Glacier. The Arm was named by Captain James Cook, who sailed here in 1778. Realizing that the fjord was not the long-sought Northwest Passage, he ordered his ships to "turn again."

Above: In the soft September light, cotton-woods display their burnished gold leaves against the primeval milieu of Kachemak Bay's Grewingk Glacier. *Right:* On the Alaska Peninsula, Hallo Creek illustrates the land-sculpting technique of the state's numerous glacial rivers. Sediment deposited by the water continually fills in streambeds, forcing the water to create new channels and to braid itself around gravel bars. *Overleaf:* Oil and natural gas were first discovered and produced on the Kenai Peninsula and Cook Inlet. Part of the North Kenai Road industrial complex, which also refines petroleum products and liquifies natural gas, the Union Chemicals plant produces ammonia and urea from natural gas for fertilizer.

Left: August wildflowers along Chiniak Inlet carpet fertile Kodiak grasslands, the year-round pasturage of livestock and wildlife. Many island residents harvest the varied riches of the surrounding sea for their livelihood. *Above:* For two years, after Japanese attacks on the Aleutian Islands during World War II, Fort Abercrombie soldiers kept vigilant watch across Kodiak's rocky shoreline to Narrow Strait and the Gulf of Alaska beyond. *Overleaf:* Passing Bull Head on the east end of Glacier Island, at the entrance to Valdez Arm, a tanker stays its course for the Valdez Marine Terminal of the trans-Alaska pipeline. There, it will take on a load of Alaskan crude.

Above: Sweeping through Shelikof Strait, the Gulf of Alaska's fierce storms bring frequent, heavy rain to Kukak Bay on the Alaska Peninsula and swell streams and waterfalls in this remote wilderness area. *Right:* As recently as the mid 1800s, 10,016-foot Mount Iliamna on the west side of Cook Inlet spewed out clouds of ash. Other nearby volcanoes remain active today. Since the early 1960s, numerous offshore rigs have tapped the oil and natural gas resource beneath the middle shoal of the 220-mile-long inlet.

Left: With tourist facilities and a deep-water port at its tip, the slender, gravel finger of Homer Spit extends four miles into Kachemak Bay. Excellent fishing, a mild climate, and spectacular scenery lure thousands of visitors each year to the "Shangri-La of Alaska." *Above:* Bordered on two sides by the silvery gray waters of Cook Inlet, Anchorage nestles against the Chugach Mountains. Three other snow-capped ranges stand close by. The wooded bluff of Earthquake Park, which commemorates the great 1964 tremor, provides this vista of downtown.

Alaska's strategic location received national attention during World War II, and the military rapidly constructed roads, airfields, and installations in the territory. Today, along with adjacent Fort Richardson, Elmendorf Air Force Base forms the headquarters for America's northern line of defense. During Armed Forces Day Open House, the public from nearby Anchorage inspects the latest military aircraft and equipment.

Above: The River Lethe cuts a gorge through the moonscape barrens of the Alaska Peninsula's Valley of Ten Thousand Smokes, a twenty-mile-long valley buried by ash and pumice during the 1912 eruption of the Mount Katmai and Novarupta volcanoes. *Overleaf:* Columbia Glacier flows forty-one miles out of the Chugach Mountains and releases icebergs which drift in the ocean currents of Prince William Sound, a scenic waterway frequented by pleasure craft and oil tankers.

Above: Once used by Natives, explorers, and gold seekers, the route over Crow Pass between Turnagain and Knik Arms attracts hikers and campers. The trail travels within the 5.9 million-acre Chugach National Forest and the adjoining 490,000-acre Chugach State Park. *Right:* Winter wind and snowscape: a rugged mountain world twenty miles from Valdez near Thompson Pass. *Overleaf:* With nearly twenty-four hours of summer daylight, Southcentral residents usually forego traditional Fourth of July fireworks. At Girdwood, a New Year's Eve display explodes above Alyeska Resort ski slopes.

Left: Each summer in a cliff-side rookery near Whittier congregate tens of thousands of black-legged Kittiwakes, a noisy delight to those who sail and cruise Passage Canal. *Above:* Herring fishermen depend on sonar as well as spotters aloft in single-engine planes to help locate schools of fish. This seiner off Gravina Point, north of Cordova, has circled its net in the water and is pulling the bottom of the net closed, trapping fish. *Overleaf:* Columbia Glacier provides an unscheduled show for tour-boat passengers by sending an explosive icefall crashing into Prince William Sound.

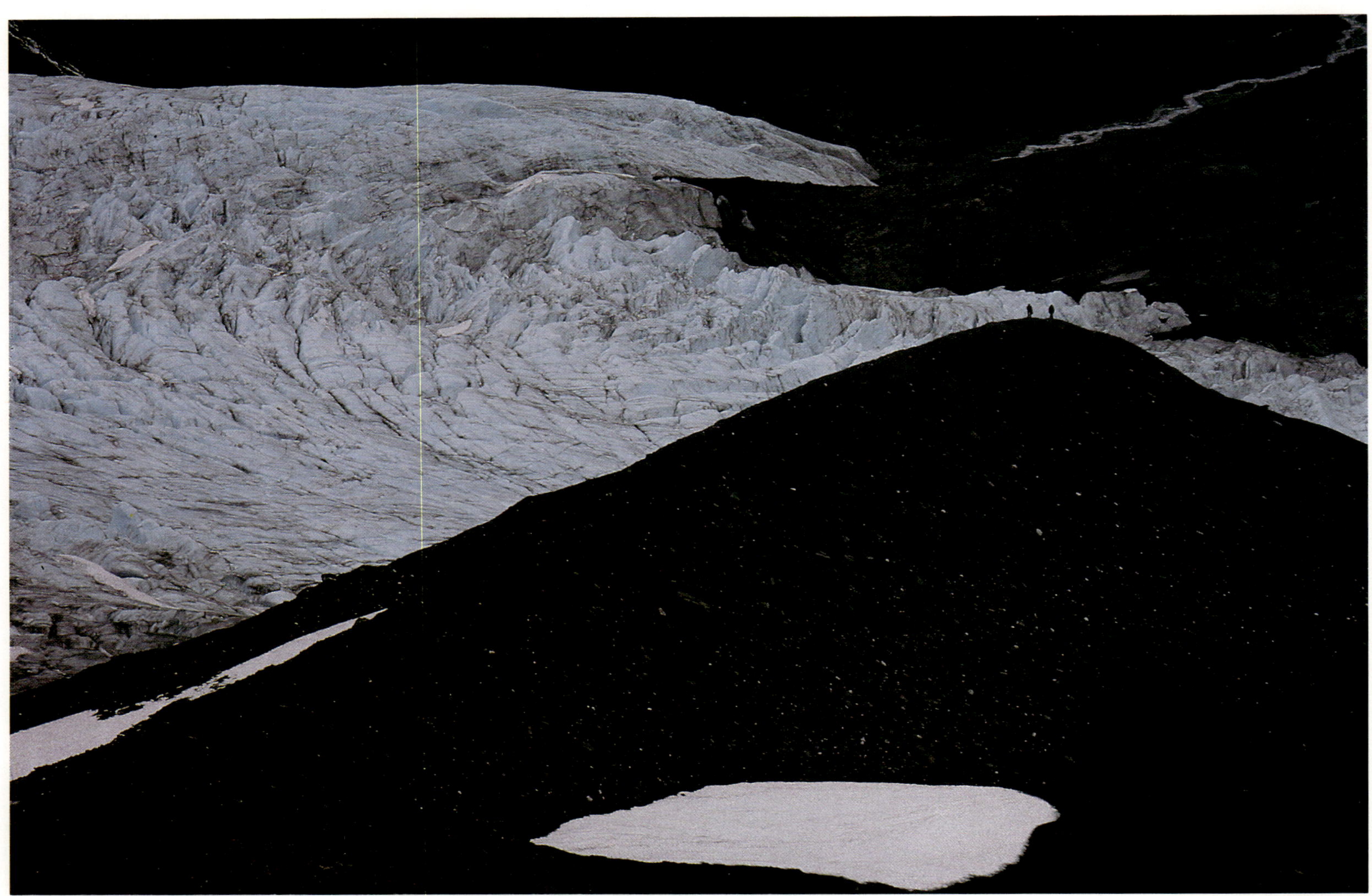

Above: The convoluted, black-veined ice of roadside Worthington Glacier entices hikers onto its hilly moraine. The Richardson Highway shares the Thompson Pass corridor with the trans-Alaska pipeline. *Right:* Alaska's Eskimo people settled the mainland coastal region from the Arctic down to Prince William Sound. The availability of subsistence resources determined the location of villages, such as Tatitlek at the base of Copper Mountain.

Left: Above timberline in Denali National Park near Cathedral Mountain, an August frost has already nipped these dwarf birch and blueberry bushes. Fall transforms the tundra into a swath of crimson sprinkled with golden thickets of willow. With summer's 80-degree Fahrenheit temperatures just past, this meadow will soon lie beneath winter's snowy blanket for the next eight months. *Above:* With the shedding of August velvet, the male caribou's antlers glow with the color of exposed blood vessels for a few hours until their surface hardens and darkens. Unlike other members of the deer family, male and female caribou *(Rangifer tarandus)* grow antlers.

Interior and Denali

Above: A young hawk owl, recently fledged in the Yukon River basin, will remain in Alaska throughout the year. Hundreds of other bird species migrate to the Interior's tundra and wetlands in summer to nest and hatch their young, then return south for the winter. *Right:* One of the world's great rivers, the 2,300-mile Yukon flows—sometimes in broad channels up to twenty miles wide—from Canada through Alaska to the Bering Sea. *Overleaf:* Wildflowers adorn a gravel bar created by glacial scouring and the sediment-laden Teklanika River.

Left: Established as a land grant institution in 1917, the 2,250-acre University of Alaska, Fairbanks campus includes the internationally acclaimed Geophysical Institute and the University of Alaska Museum. The UAF Agricultural Station develops special north country hybrids ranging from corn to roses. *Above:* Now a restaurant, the pump house of the Fairbanks Exploration Company provided water for gold-dredging operations east of Fairbanks during the 1930s. *Overleaf:* Powerful electrical storms sweep across the vast Interior during the summer. Paved for a quarter of its one hundred and sixty miles, the Steese Highway connects Fairbanks with the town of Circle on the Yukon River.

Above: Beckoning through the darkness of a winter afternoon, lights illuminate a log cabin at Alaskaland, Fairbanks' pioneer park of historic buildings, shops, dance halls and theaters, restaurants and playgrounds. *Right:* Centuries of irresistable pressure by advancing walls of ice created the Great Gorge of the Ruth Glacier. More than twenty glaciers flowing from the Mount McKinley massif measure five to forty miles in length. *Overleaf:* Sentry duty rotates among members of this band of Dall Sheep (*Ovis dalli dalli*) who inhabit the high ranges of Denali National Park. The six million-acre park is home to thirty-seven mammal species and one hundred and thirty species of birds.

Left: Barely rising above the southern horizon, the noon sun filters through ice-fog shrouding the Interior's low-land community of North Pole. On minus 45-degree December days, numerous layers of loose clothing provide the best outdoor protection for people, while electric engine and battery heaters help vehicles start in sub-zero temperatures. *Above:* Ten miles southeast of Fairbanks, steam columns rise from the oil refinery which produces heating oil, diesel fuel, aviation kerosene, and asphalt from Prudhoe Bay oil.

Above: The 2 A.M. July ground-fog obscuring the Kanuti River flats will burn off later in the nightless day as the sun rises. At approximately 66° 33' north of the equator, the Arctic Circle is an imaginary arc across the top third of Alaska. The line marks the southernmost latitude where the sun does not set during the summer solstice and where, during the winter solstice, it does not rise. *Right:* The George Parks Highway linking Anchorage and Fairbanks crosses the Alaska Range over Broad Pass. At an elevation of 2,300 feet, this pass is one of the lowest divides in the North American highway system. On its north side, rivers like the Jack, drain into the Yukon; rivers on the south side flow into Cook Inlet.

Left: Sweet-tooth satisfiers. Bears devour tangy wild blueberries complete with stems and leaves, while Alaskans harvest this low bush fruit for pies, preserves, sauces, and salads. *Above:* Few bridges span streams and rivers in Alaska's wilderness, and the frigid glacial waters present a tricky challenge to hikers. This adventurer aims for a dry landing on the other side of a Teklanika River channel. *Overleaf:* Climbers carry their gear to an air taxi waiting on the packed-snow runway of Kahilta Glacier's "international airport." Mount McKinley's south face looms in the center background.

N1062F

Above: For more than ten years, Frances Randall has spent her spring managing the Kahiltna Glacier base camp and her winters playing violin with the Fairbanks Symphony Orchestra. *Right:* All the comforts of home, except perhaps hot running water; the base camp radio room relays rapidly changing weather information to bush pilots as well as emergency messages about lost, sick, or injured climbers. *Overleaf:* Dog-mushing enthusiasts keep part of Alaska's romantic past alive. The state's official sport attracts fans to numerous local and statewide races. The more notable ones are the North American in Fairbanks, Anchorage's World Championship, and the 1,049-mile Iditarod from Anchorage to Nome.

KAHILTNA
NATIONAL
FOREST

Left: Mastodon Dome stands silhouetted on the horizon near the Steese Highway north of Fairbanks. Layers upon layers of these low rolling hills march across the central Interior. *Above:* A private residence in Fairbanks, Alaska's second largest city, which lies in the vast Tanana River Valley. Begun after a gold discovery in 1903, the community boomed as the supply source for nearby mining activity. Today, it remains a supply and service center for Interior and Arctic industrial activities. *Overleaf:* When Alaska was Russian, the great crest was known as Bulshaia Gora, "Big Mountain." The Americans who purchased the territory in 1867 named the lofty peak for the United States' twenty-fifth President, William McKinley. Most Alaskans call it Denali, the Tanaina Indian word for "High One."

Above: Success at last for one team on Denali's 20,320-foot South Peak. The mountain actually consists of two peaks: the 19,470-foot North Peak, first climbed by two prospectors in 1910, and the South Peak, conquered three years later. *Right:* Inupiat Eskimos at Wainwright haul in a bowhead whale using blocks left by whaling ships which plied Arctic waters during the early 1900s.

Western Alaska, Arctic, and the Aleutians

Left: July's midnight sun blazes along the silent carrier of Alaska's "black gold," traveling south from the oil wells of Prudhoe Bay. Completed in 1977, the pipeline stretches eight hundred miles across three mountain ranges and hundreds of rivers and streams to tankers waiting at Valdez. Refined on the East and Gulf coasts, Prudhoe crude oil supplies about one-seventh of America's daily requirement. *Above:* Tundra jack-in-the-box: a Brooks Range ground squirrel surveys its tundra world, ready to utter a piercing warning whistle to its companion if danger threatens.

Remnants of two civilizations lie along the Nome-Council road on the southern Seward Peninsula. Saucer-shaped earthen depressions mark the ancient locations of three hundred Native dwellings, while the rusting hulk of Solomon's narrow-gauge railroad recalls the area's glory days of gold in the early 1900s. Today, Native corporations team up with major international companies to explore Northwestern Alaska's myriad mineral resources.

Above: Two hundred and thirty miles south of Prudhoe Bay in the Brooks Range, Wiseman's rough log cabins once housed gold miners during the town's 1910 heyday. Isolated for years, Wiseman's year-round population of four suddenly saw the world passing its doorstep as the trans-Alaska pipeline was constructed on the opposite side of the Koyukuk River. *Overleaf:* Far from supermarkets and convenience stores, Bush residents must be skillful in providing for their own needs.

Above: Rural Alaska's changing life-style: utility poles and dories line the Arctic Ocean waterfront of Kotzebue, whose predominantly Eskimo population of three thousand depends mainly on subsistence and commercial fishing and Native corporation ventures, such as reindeer herding and jade mining. *Right:* Snowmachines and three-wheelers have almost replaced the traditional dog team for ground transportation in the Bush. *Overleaf:* Both clothes and moose meat dry outside a Kotzebue residence in September.

Left: A freighter approaches Amaknak Island's Dutch Harbor, an important service stop along international shipping lanes. Creating constantly changing weather, frigid Bering Sea and warm Japanese currents collide along the 1,100-mile Aleutian archipelago, nicknamed "birthplace of the wind." *Above:* Eskimos attending Barrow's Utkeagvik Presbyterian Church sing from a hymnal written in Inupiat, their Native language, which most use interchangeably with English. *Overleaf:* The 1899 discovery of gold on a desolate beach launched a stampede: Nome exploded into existence the next summer with a population of thirty thousand, half of whom left discouraged later that fall. With gold's increasing world price, dredges like this one on the Seward Peninsula and mining operations around the state have become active again.

Above: In 1741, Captain Vitus Bering sighted the Aleutian Islands and claimed them for the Czar of Russia. Luxurious pelts brought back by his crew set off a "soft gold" rush, and Russians enslaved the local Aleut people to hunt fur seals, driving both people and animal to the brink of extinction. Among the Aleut people today, the Russian Orthodox faith, exemplified by Unalaska's onion-domed Holy Ascension of Christ church, remains strong. *Right:* The treeless, grassy mountains of the Aleutians form biological stepping-stones between the continents of Asia and North America. Vegetation and seventy-nine bird species of Asian origin are found on the western islands, while on the eastern islands are found plant life and one hundred and fifty species of birds common to North America.

Left: Brisk winds swirl dry snow around cross-country skiers descending Angiaak Pass during an April expedition in the Brooks Range. Much of this Range and the rest of Alaska—about 155.7 million acres in all—lie within state or federal park boundaries. *Above:* June in the Brooks Range: The silver trans-Alaska pipeline threads over frozen tundra along the base of Slope Mountain. Extensive environmental studies before pipeline construction resulted in design considerations which accommodated migrating caribou, hibernating bears, mountain sheep during the lambing season, and nesting peregrine falcons.

Above: Playful and inquisitive, red and cross fox kits peer out on their world near the Chandalar River. Alaska's Native people traditionally viewed their subsistence life-style as a partnership: the land and animals provided food and clothing; by living there, the people gave the land life. *Right:* Lupine and a rainbow of wildflowers and grasses thrive year-round in the Aleutians' moist climate and average mid-30s to mid-50s Fahrenheit temperatures. *Overleaf:* Blanketing Alaska's boggy marshes with summertime white, the soft cotton grass can be dried to make delicate bouquets.

Left: Slippery footing: frozen spray coats rocks near an Atigun Pass waterfall in June. Constant wind through the Brooks Range keeps most mountainsides fairly snow-free and exposes forage for Dall sheep. *Above:* At the NANA Museum of the Arctic in Kotzebue, young Eskimos recreate traditional dances for visitors, while village elders beat time on sealskin drums. Along with rural Alaska's headlong rush into modernization and a cash-economy has come a resurgence of cultural pride among the state's original peoples. *Overleaf:* American servicemen stationed at Dutch Harbor during World War II watched for Japanese invaders from bunkers above Iliuliuk Bay.

Above: May's midnight light reveals bowhead whales surfacing just yards away from Eskimo hunters, who ready their traditional sealskin boat, the "umiaq," for the chase. *Right:* A sun halo warns of an impending weather change for the Alatna River. The rivers of roadless, rural Alaska serve as highways—for winter skiers, dog mushers, and snowmobilers, and for summer boaters, canoers, and kayakers. *Overleaf:* Swollen with July's meltwater, a glacial creek tumbles down a granite staircase near Arrigetch Peaks. The Eskimos named the peaks, a fan-shaped array of fiercely sheer granite spires, "arrigetch," the "outstretched fingers of the hand."

Left: Scientists believe the eerie Aurora Borealis results from charged solar particles which, striking the earth's atmosphere, create colored lights. Ancient Native legends say the undulating Northern Lights come from torches lighting the way to heaven for departed souls. *Above:* Though little snow falls in the arid Arctic overall, howling winter winds pack drifts up to the rooftops. These Kotzebue children scrambled up nature's walkway to one of the highest spots in town—a perfect place to frolic.